Mother Christmas' Journey

£6.95

Mother Christmas' Journey

Mary Martin and Valerie Stumbles

Cassell

Cassell Educational Limited
Artillery House, Artillery Row, London SW1P 1RT

© 1987 by Cassell Educational Limited

First published 1987

ISBN 0 304 31413 7

Illustrations by Bob Tyndall

British Library Cataloguing in Publication Data
Martin, Mary
  Mother Christmas' journey.
  I. Title II. Stumbles, Valerie
  823'.914[J]   PZ7

Printed by The Alden Press, Oxford

PREFACE

Christmas ideas usually flow quite readily, so we make no excuse for
borrowing the two most prominent and sandwiching them together!
Father Christmas has always been a children's favourite and the Nativity,
the heart of all Christmas. Combine the two and add a few simple
melodies and hopefully we have a performance that brings laughter and
joy to all ages. We should like to dedicate this book to all who believe the
spirit of Christmas should live on!

'Is nothing going to go right this year?' sighed Mother Christmas as she removed her second batch of crumbly mince pies from the oven. Just as she was about to cry, Father Christmas appeared from his workshop. 'What's the matter dear?' he said. 'Nothing really', said Mother Christmas. 'But after all the years of practice I've had baking for Christmas, I've made a real disaster of this one!' 'Oh, is that all?', said Father Christmas. He paused for a moment and then said 'I'll give you a Christmas to remember. Instead of staying home this year, would you come with me and deliver the presents?'

1. Leave the cooking

Leave the cook-ing, leave the clean-ing, leave the pots and pans. Come with me to-night. Make some fac - es

bright Mo-ther Christ-mas. Girls and boys will be in bed. Gent-ly kiss them

on their heads. Smile a smile and all will see Christ-mas-es in to E - ter - nit - y.

(No percussion)

7

Mother Christmas dried her eyes and a smile crept across her face. It might be nice to see the world from up above for the first time. Father and Mother Christmas took the next day to get ready for their mammoth trek around the world. Mother Christmas took with them a small picnic basket full of crumbly mince pies. They climbed aboard the sleigh and headed into the distance very quickly.

2. Hurry, hurry, hurry

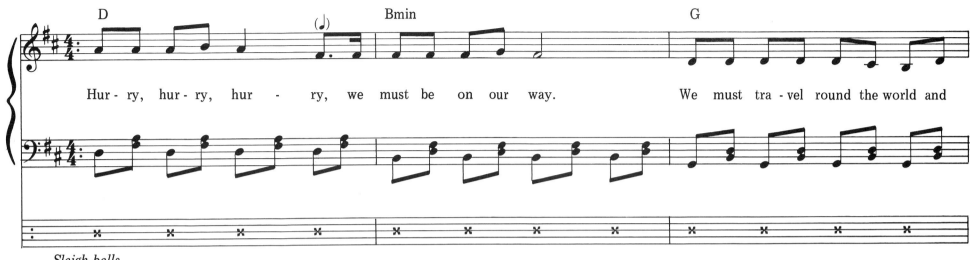

Sleigh bells

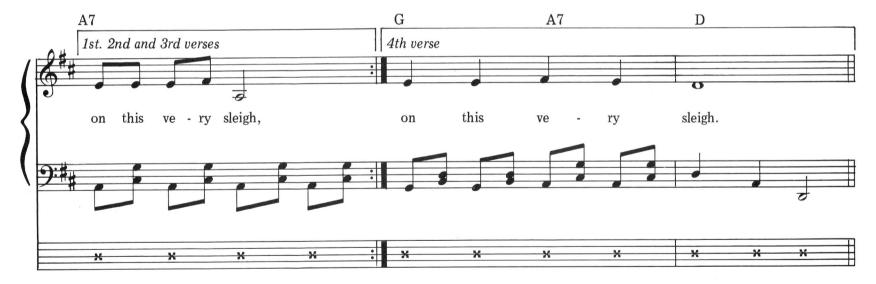

(Percussion: Sleigh bells)

v.2. Hurry, hurry, hurry. We must not delay.
We must travel round the world.
We can't take all day.

v.3. Over snow clad roof tops, under bridges tall,
We have travelled round the world
Over every wall.

9

Within seconds Mother Christmas found herself over ice packs and icebergs and looking down on polar bears playing in the moonshine. Very gently Father Christmas guided the sleigh down onto the snow laden ground beneath. 'Here we are then, first stop, Northern Canada.'

3. They don't throw snowballs here anymore

(Glockenspiel)

(Percussion: Glockenspiel)

Mother Christmas saw a village made of igloos. She watched Father Christmas rub noses with an Eskimo dad. 'It makes my nose so sore', he said. 'Where to now?' said Mother Christmas when he returned to the sleigh. 'The United States of America!' came the reply. The sleigh bells echoed through the high buildings telling New York that Santa was well and truly on his way.

4. Skyscraper maze

Sky-scra-per maze ___ you're driv-ing me cra - zy ___ Sky-scra-per maze ___ I don't know where I

am. Al-though it's New York ci - ty that's ver - y clear. They

don't have sign - posts way up here. How can I de - liv - er pre - sents ___ to

all the boys and girls? How can I find ad - dress - es in this con - crete world?

(No percussion)

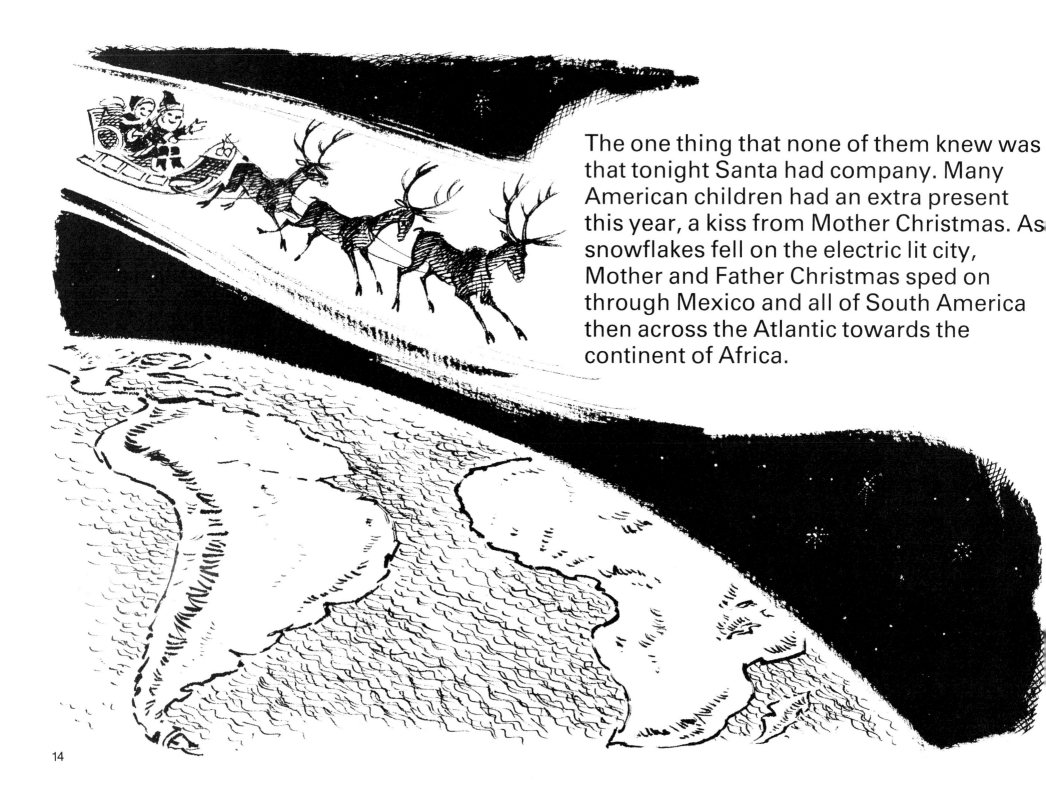

The one thing that none of them knew was that tonight Santa had company. Many American children had an extra present this year, a kiss from Mother Christmas. As snowflakes fell on the electric lit city, Mother and Father Christmas sped on through Mexico and all of South America then across the Atlantic towards the continent of Africa.

5. Listen to the talking drums

Lis-ten to the talk - ing drums say-ing he comes, he comes.

Bongos

Lis - ten to the jun - gle mu - sic go-ing all a - cross this land. This is how they wel - come

San - ta in this sun - baked land. Lis - ten to the talk - ing drums say -ing he

comes, he comes. comes _____ he comes.

(Percussion: Bongos)

15

Mother Christmas squealed with delight as she saw lots of jungle creatures. When they had delivered all the presents to the villages, they set off southwards towards the world's largest island. They soon arrived in Australia.

6. Koala bear, Kangaroo

(No percussion - Wobble board(?) à la Rolf Harris(?))

Leaving Australia the couple headed towards Europe and sped on to visit Germany, France, Holland, Denmark, Austria, Sweden, and Norway. The night seemed to be going very quickly. Father Christmas then pointed to the lights beneath them. 'Look!' he said.

7. I have travelled the world

I have tra-velled the world ov-er ma-ny years but Lon-don's a won-der-ful sight. Some-how it ne-ver seems differ-ent, it's quite a friend of mine. I can call for tea with the Queen you know. I can match the guard so fine. I can talk to Nel-son on top of his col-umn and ask Big Ben the time. I have tra-velled the world ov-er ma-ny years but Lon-don's a won-der-ful sight.

Chime bars

(Percussion: Chime bars D A G)

Finally, Father Christmas took out his notebook and struck off the very last address. He gave an immense yawn as they started homeward. Mother Christmas looked at his tired face. It told a story and this year she had been a part of it.

8. All aboard we're homeward bound

Sleigh bells

v.2. Take us through the starlit sky
Through the Milky Way.
We must hurry homeward,
Tomorrow's Christmas day.

v.3. We've delivered presents
To every sleeping child.
Tomorrow they'll remember
Jesus the Holy Child.

(Percussion: Sleigh bells)

Mother Christmas found her eyes shutting. She was soon dreaming, but she awoke with a start. 'Oh, dear', she said. 'We've forgotten to visit Bethlehem.'
'Can't have done', said Father Christmas. 'There's not a thing left in the sack!'
'We've some crumbly mince pies.' They very soon found themselves sailing over the minarets of Bethlehem.

9. Bethlehem

Beth-le-hem, Beth-le-hem where a babe was born. Beth-le-hem, Beth-le-hem

Glockenspiel *Chime bars* *Glockenspiel*

on a Christ-mas morn. Beth-le-hem, Beth-le-hem how did you

Chime bars *Glockenspiel* *Chime bars*

hide a lit-tle babe a new born king, so swell-ing with pride?

Fine *D.C. al Fine*
Piano only

(Percussion: Glockenspiel (F♯, E, D) Chime bars [D/B/G] [E/C♯/A] [A/F♯/D])

v.2. Bethlehem, Bethlehem
Lying fast asleep,
Bethlehem, Bethlehem
Can we come to peep?

Bethlehem, Bethlehem
Can we see the boy
A little babe
A new born king
Our pride and joy?

23

The sleigh gently came to a halt outside an inn in Bethlehem. In the distance they could see a caravan of camels heading towards them. They suddenly realised what had happened. Not only had they travelled miles but also back in time.

'Are you thinking what I am thinking?' said Father Christmas.

'Mmm' said Mother Christmas. 'I think we'd better wait' continued Father Christmas. 'They had better arrive first.'

10. I think we'd better wait

(Percussion: Indian bells)

Three kings arrived in procession bearing special gifts. The door of the inn swung open and a wonderous sight befell them. Mary and Joseph smiled a welcome. Mother Christmas nudged Father Christmas to give the happy couple the crumbly mince pies. 'This has really made my Christmas', whispered Mother Christmas and she squeezed her husband's arm. Father Christmas nodded in agreement as they quietly returned to their sleigh for the return journey.

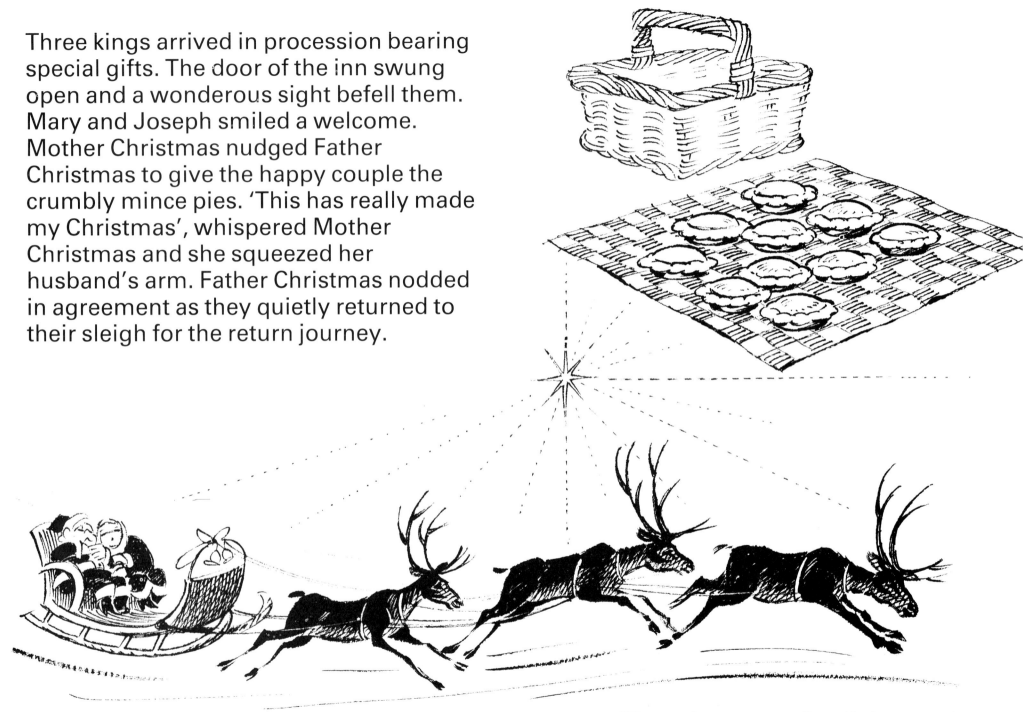

They slept soundly all the way home.

11. Sing, sing, sing

(No percussion)

v.2. Shepherds leaving the new born sheep sleeping
Went on their knees a-peeping
Sent by an angel of love.
Wise men, travelling miles across hot sands
Visiting all the new lands
Come to see the new born king.   Sing, Sing, Sing.

v.3. Angels soon made the heavens all ringing
Filling the skies with their singing
Singing to the new born king.
Jesus, lying there softly in a manger
New born king but a stranger
King of all the world.   Sing, Sing, Sing.

Mother Christmas' Journey

'Is nothing going to go right this year?' sighed Mother Christmas as she removed her second batch of crumbly mince pies from the oven. To date, her puff pastry hadn't puffed, her Christmas cake weighed a ton and the fruit had sunk to the bottom, and to top it all, her Christmas pudding would not turn out of the basin!

Just as she was sighing another sigh and about to shed a tear, Father Christmas appeared from his workshop. 'What's the matter dear?' he said in a caring tone. 'Feeling under the weather?'

'Not really', sobbed Mother Christmas, 'but after all the practice I've had baking for Christmas, I've made a real disaster of this one!' 'Oh is that all?' said Father Christmas. 'Don't give it another thought.' He paused for a moment and then said, 'I'll give you a Christmas to remember. Instead of staying at home this year, come with me and deliver the presents. I'm sure you'll enjoy yourself.'

Mother Christmas dried her eyes and a smile crept across her face. It might be nice to see the world from up above for the first time!

Father and Mother Christmas spent the next day getting ready for their mammoth trek around the world. Father Christmas gave the reindeer extra oats and carrots to prepare them for their journey. Finally he loaded all the toys on board his sleigh. He carefully folded a sleigh rug on the seat next to his own, ready to protect Mother Christmas' knees from the cold night air, and with a little chuckle to himself he summoned her with a hearty 'Are you ready then?'

When Mother Christmas arrived on the scene she was dressed up in her best clothes and was carrying a small picnic basket containing a few crumbly mince pies. Father Christmas wrapped the sleigh rug around her knees and with a gentle 'Come on' his sleigh rose upwards and headed into the distance at a speed Concorde could not match! Within seconds Mother Christmas found herself flying over ice packs and icebergs and looking down on polar bears playing in the moonshine. Having left her stomach back at home at take off Mother Christmas was feeling somewhat travel sick. She swallowed hard and to her own amazement the feeling began to pass. Very gently Father Christmas guided the sleigh down onto the snow laden ground beneath. 'Here we are then' he said. 'First stop, Northern Canada.'

Mother Christmas found herself staring at a village made of ice houses called igloos. She watched her husband crawling in and out of the icy tunnels delivering presents. She watched him rub noses with an Eskimo dad. 'Strange custom' she said to Father Christmas as he returned to the sleigh. 'Yes' agreed Father Christmas. 'I'm glad most of them are in bed. It makes my nose so sore!' Mother Christmas couldn't resist picking up a handful of snow and throwing it at Father Christmas. 'Hey, no time for that!' he said. 'Where to now then?' enquired Mother Christmas.

'I'll give you a clue', said Father Christmas and with that he sang a chorus of 'Yankee Doodle Dandy'. Mother Christmas covered her ears. 'Mmm' she said soothingly, 'The United States of America'. Rudolph and the other reindeer sprinted over snow clad roof tops and in and out of the skyscrapers. The sound of the sleigh bells echoed between the high buildings telling the sleeping city that Santa was well and truly on his way. The one thing that none of them knew was that this year Santa had company. The United States slept soundly as Father Christmas and his wife delivered presents in double quick time. Many children had an extra special present this year, a kiss from Mother Christmas!

As snowflakes fell on the electric lit towers Mother and Father Christmas sped through Mexico and all of South America. Cape Horn was a little stormy and Mother Christmas began to worry. 'Gee up, my beauties!' said Father Christmas, and with a flash of their heels, sleigh and reindeer whisked across the Atlantic towards Africa.

As the bright red sun sank beneath the horizon, Mother Christmas squeezed Father Christmas' arm and squealed with delight. 'Oh look' she said. 'There's a giraffe, and a lion, and a gazelle and a leopard and ....' 'I know dear' said Father Christmas. 'They were here last year and the year before that and the year before that ....' 'Isn't it exciting though?'

continued Mother Christmas. Having delivered all the presents to all the children scattered about the great continent, Mother Christmas settled back down in the sleigh and watched as desert, jungle and grassland passed beneath her.

The sleigh headed southwards across the Indian Ocean in search of the world's largest island, Australia. They arrived early and Mother Christmas spent a few hours on the beach watching surfers ride the huge waves. Although very tempted to have a try she felt she wasn't dressed properly, so they waited till dusk and then began their deliveries. Mother Christmas was amazed at how far they had to travel to each township and told Father Christmas that she wasn't surprised that kangaroos had to hop everywhere! As they flew over Sydney Mother Christmas was intrigued to see the huge opera house and asked Father Christmas if they might stop. 'I'm in too much of a hurry, I'm afraid', said Father Christmas, 'perhaps I'll bring you another time.'

Without further ado they flew on at great speed to visit Europe. They went through Germany, Austria, Holland and France. The night seemed to be going so quickly, already the first signs of the dawn waking were filling the skies. 'Look dear!' said Father Christmas, 'My favourite town, London.' Mother Christmas was given a conducted tour of London and told all about the sights. The Houses of Parliament, Big Ben, Buckingham Palace, Trafalgar Square. Father Christmas cheekily waved to Nelson and went on chuckling to himself and delivering presents as fast as he could. Finally he took out his notebook and struck off the last address. 'Well my dear, home to bed and a cup of cocoa.' 'Lovely' said Mother Christmas. 'We've been around the world in less time than it takes me to bake our Christmas cake!'

Father Christmas gave an immense yawn as they set off homeward. Mother Christmas looked at him lovingly. His tired face told a story and this year she had been a part of it. Boys and girls the world over had longed to see her husband, but once again he had sped into the night without a careless footstep. She tucked the sleigh rug around his knees and leaned gently against him.

Mother Christmas found her eyes closing and soon she began to dream. She awoke with a start. 'Oh, my dear, my dear' she repeated to a startled Father Christmas. 'We've not visited Bethlehem.' 'I can't have forgotten anybody, there's not a present left in the sack', replied Father Christmas.

'But we have', insisted Mother Christmas, 'and I do have some crumbly mince pies.'

'Double speed, Rudolph!' commanded Father Christmas and with supersonic speed they found themselves sailing over the minarets of Bethlehem. They flew over the actual city and came to rest outside an inn. The night was still, and the air cool. The sky was lit by a thousand stars brighter than Mother Christmas had ever seen before. 'Oh dear', said Mother Christmas. 'It's sort of eerie!' Father Christmas tried to comfort her but he felt strange. In the distance he could see a camel caravan. It was heading towards them and suddenly he realised what had happened. Not only had they travelled miles but they had travelled back in time. 'Are you thinking what I'm thinking, Mother Christmas?' he asked. 'Mmm' she said trembling. 'We'd better wait', he continued. 'They had better arrive first.'

Three kings arrived in procession bearing special gifts. The door of the inn swung open and a wonderful sight befell them. Mary and Joseph smiled a welcome. Mother and Father Christmas were speechless. When Mother Christmas came to her senses she nudged Father Christmas to give the happy couple the crumbly mince pies.

Father Christmas mumbled something about the fact that it was not his custom to forget people at this time of the year but he had been caught unawares. The couple smiled. Father Christmas coughed uncomfortably. 'This has really made my Christmas!' squealed Mother Christmas. Father Christmas nodded in agreement as they quietly returned to their sleigh for the long journey home.

They slept soundly all the way.